Original title:
Life's Puzzle: Missing a Few Pieces

Copyright © 2025 Creative Arts Management OÜ
All rights reserved.

Author: Simon Fairchild
ISBN HARDBACK: 978-1-80566-220-4
ISBN PAPERBACK: 978-1-80566-515-1

Echoes of What Once Was

In a box, so many bits,
My cat thinks they're her toys.
I chase memories, throw a fit,
While she ponders life's joys.

Images of yesterday,
Are scattered all around.
Can't find the pieces to play,
But laugh at the lost sound.

Mosaic of Unfinished Stories

A jigsaw without corners,
Pieces shaped like chicken legs.
These tales have no forewarnings,
Just thoughts that twist and beg.

Each fragment a funny tale,
Of mishaps and silly fall.
Can't find the end of the trail,
But humor rules over all.

The Beauty of Imperfection

Art from misfit colors bright,
Who needs a match, or a plan?
In chaos, I find pure delight,
As laughter stirs from a can.

The round peg in square holes giggles,
Each funny twist feels just right.
Stumbling through life's little wiggles,
It's all about joy in the fight.

Navigating the Unknown

A map with lines all askew,
Still, I wander, not a care.
With every turn, something new,
While Google Maps pulls its hair.

Lost in thoughts, but what a ride,
A compass with no direction.
With every wrong turn, I glide,
And chuckle at my own reflection.

The Art of Incomplete Journeys

In a suitcase, I packed my dreams,
Forgot my socks, or so it seems.
The map's upside down, what a sight!
Chasing directions, it feels so right.

Bumpy roads make for funny tales,
Where every wrong turn reveals odd trails.
I skipped the guide, read the back instead,
Now I'm lost, but I'm not misled.

Café chairs and awkward chats,
In a foreign land with cats as bureaucrats.
Signs in languages I can't decode,
Yet I follow the nudge of my whimsied road.

At a crossroads, I stood so wise,
But the ice cream shop stole my eyes.
Flip a coin, heads or tails,
Either works, let's savor our fails.

Chasing Shadows of Yesterday

In yesterday's shades, I roam quite far,
Chasing memories like a shooting star.
I bought a ticket, yet missed the train,
Found a stray dog, who also felt the same.

We play hide and seek, with shadows that shift,
Every corner turned reveals a gift.
A sandwich half-eaten, still on the ground,
Perhaps the universe wants to astound.

Why'd I wear mismatched shoes today?
They're stylish, I loudly declare, with a sway.
One's a bright red, one's a dull gray,
Is it fashion or folly? Who's to say?

The ghosts of my past offer advice,
But trip on the stairs, not once, but thrice.
Yet laughter erupts while I tumble down,
In this dance with time, I'll never frown.

Embracing the Unfamiliar

In a land where the cows roam free,
I asked for directions; they laughed at me.
With a wink and a nod, they gestured wide,
I set off boldly, with a quirky guide.

Street food stalls with strange delight,
Mysterious dishes that give quite a fright.
I'll try the jelly, the squishy green square,
What if it wiggles? Who really cares?

At the market, I bartered my shoe,
For a statue that looked remarkably blue.
A fine trade, if I say so myself,
Now it sits proudly, right on my shelf.

New customs, new faces, all feel so odd,
But each moment feels like an adventure abroad.
So here's to the quirky, the strange, and the new,
Where laughter's the language, and fun's the glue.

Threads of a Tattered Map

Oh dear map, frayed through the years,
Identifying locations through countless cheers.
X marks the spot, or so they say,
But today it points to a cafe buffet.

I wander through streets both bustling and bare,
Waving at strangers who really don't care.
I trip over roots, dance with the breeze,
While counting the leaves on the nearby trees.

My compass spins wildly, a game gone amok,
I follow my heart, and the friendly flock.
They teach me to tango under the sun,
In this upside-down voyage, it's all in good fun.

With every misstep, I shrug and I grin,
For every lost moment is an invitation in.
Threads of a tattered map unfold in delight,
Leading to laughter from morning to night.

Unwoven Tales

In a shoebox full of socks,
I found a toy rubber duck.
It quacked and danced a strange jig,
Guess it was out of luck.

My toaster speaks in riddles,
The kettle hums a tune.
Together they plot my breakfast,
At a very odd noon.

Each shoe lost its partner,
In the great laundry fight.
Now I wear mismatched sneakers,
In bold colors so bright.

The cat steals all my pencils,
To write her feline prose.
While I search for my missing keys,
She stares at me and dozes.

Searching for the Unknown

I lost my wallet somewhere,
Under the couch, it might be.
Or perhaps it went on vacation,
To an island, carefree.

My left sock's a runaway,
Joining a sock puppet team.
While I sit here, quite confused,
Stuck in a mismatched dream.

The remote has taken cover,
Draped in a blanket's sway.
Maybe it's seeking freedom,
From the binge-watching play.

I chased the fridge's humming,
Thinking secrets it might tell.
Instead, it just laughed at me,
With the milk that went sour as well.

Glimpses of the Unsung

Missed a piece of breakfast,
Eggs dancing on the plate.
Pancakes ran away laughing,
It seems they've sealed my fate.

The clock has lost its ticking,
It's gone on a short spree.
I ask it for directions,
But time is never free.

The spaghetti's twisted tales,
They weave through sauce so bright.
Yet every fork I pick up,
Just twirls into a fight.

My mug dreams of adventures,
With spoons who sail so far.
While I sit here, quite puzzled,
By this missing sugar jar.

The Half-Drawn Map

I drew a map of treasure,
But forgot to label 'X!'
Now I'm lost in my own yard,
Pondering my old hex.

The compass spins in circles,
It's dizzy with its quest.
It points towards the cookie jar,
Where crumbs are quite the guest.

A pirate's hat is missing,
I guess it went out to sea.
And now I'm wearing sunglasses,
Feeling like a shark, whee!

Each step feels like a riddle,
Hidden within the leaves.
Searching for bits of laughter,
Missing in all their heaves.

Mismatched Connections

A sock lost in the laundry dance,
A partner in the tango, missing chance.
Filled with hope, we try to blend,
Yet oddities seem to be our trend.

A puzzle piece stuck to your shoe,
Wonders to know just how it flew.
Each twist and turn, a giggle ensues,
In this game, even clowns can lose.

The Void Between

Where's my sandwich? You ate it whole!
Your appetite's a bottomless hole.
With crumbs as clues, I search the way,
In this void, laughter leads the stray.

A cat who steals my sunny spot,
He rolls and purrs, too snug to trot.
We navigate this silly spree,
Amidst the gaps, we find our glee.

A Walk Among the Shadows

Stumbling on shadows, what a sight,
They dance and tease in the fading light.
I trip on laughter, the ghost of glee,
As shadows whisper, 'Come, dance with me!'

With mismatched shoes, I waddle along,
Each step a note to an unfinished song.
The silliness echoes, so sweet and bright,
These absent pieces, a pure delight.

Unfinished Symphonies

In a world where notes play hide and seek,
My trumpet honks; the violin's weak.
We laugh and fumble through the jest,
With missing notes, it's still the best.

An orchestra of giggles, we create,
Each misshapen tune we celebrate.
With every flub, we find new ways,
Who needs perfection when fun's the craze?

Reaching for the Unreachable

I stretched my arms to the sky,
Hoping for something nearby.
A donut maybe, or a shoe,
Turns out I'm just reaching for you.

The coffee pot's my greatest foe,
It's empty now, what a show.
I dance around with hope anew,
But trips and spills, is that on you?

I skidded past the cat with grace,
He barely even turned his face.
Did he see my fumbled pride?
Or is he judging from outside?

So here I am, in clumsy cheer,
With socks that clash, loud and clear.
Yet still I leap, still I try,
To catch the dreams that float up high.

Heartbeats in the Gaps

There's a knock, who can it be?
A missing sock, a lost cup of tea.
And there I stand, flipping through the pile,
Coughing up the giggles with a smile.

I check my phone, it's just a glow,
No message sent, just here we go.
In silence, I dance, a merry chase,
Counting heartbeat gaps, let's embrace.

The cat's opinion, oh so acute,
As he judges my strange pursuit.
While I search for joy in all things slight,
He yawns and curls up tight tonight.

In these pauses, laughter grows,
Between the ticks, we all know.
Life's funny, with quirks like grace,
Heartbeats glimpsed, a warm embrace.

The Elusive Second Chance

I knocked on doors that just won't budge,
Chasing down dreams I wouldn't begrudge.
But oh, they giggle as they pass by,
Now I need a map, oh my-oh-my!

I ponder chances like they're rare coins,
Flipping them round, oh, what do I want?
Heads, I try again, tails, I just laugh,
And with every hoot, I learn to half-staff.

They say the early bird catches the worm,
But what about those who love to squirm?
With breakfast gone, I have to pretend,
That brunch is just breakfast, my dear friend.

So here's to chances that slip and slide,
The laughter shared, the joy worldwide.
In every misstep, a jig and a dance,
A second glimpse, a wild romance.

Searching for the Fragments

I'm sifting through my mixed-up sock drawer,
What treasures lie behind each door?
Oh look, a pencil, dusty and old,
With tales forgotten, too shy to be told.

I peek inside my memory's well,
With echoes of laughter, can you tell?
Did we play hide-and-seek, or was that a dream?
Fragments of giggles, bursting at the seam.

A puzzle piece from yesterday's snack,
Pops out and says, 'Hey, I want back!'
Sandwich crusts turn into art displays,
As I search for joy in silly ways.

So here I sit amidst the debris,
Smiling at all the things that be.
In fragments lost, I find the thread,
Weaving a tapestry of joy, widespread.

In Search of the Invisible

Where's that sock? It had a mate,
Hiding from the laundry fate.
Keys are lost, the wallet's shy,
Guess it's time to say goodbye!

Thought I saw my phone just there,
Oh wait, it's in my purple chair.
Fridge is empty, not a snack,
Only ghosts of dinners past, we lack!

Chasing shadows, catching air,
Everywhere, but nowhere, where?
A puzzle piece, it slipped away,
In the realm of 'not today.'

But laughter comes to ease the stress,
As we embrace this chaotic mess.
For in the search, we find the fun,
Invisible treasures, one by one!

Faded Echoes

Old memories, they fade and slip,
Like my grip on this coffee cup.
Laughter lingers in the hall,
But echoes seem to have a ball.

Once I danced like a carefree breeze,
Now I trip over my own cheese.
Bright days dimmed by cloudy minds,
The silly truth is what one finds.

Time's a joker, can't you see?
With every tick, it plays with me.
A puzzle half done brings a grin,
Missing pieces caused by my din.

So let's toast to fumbles and jests,
Every stumble becomes our best.
For in this play of give and take,
We find the fun in every mistake!

The Unraveling Tapestry

Threads come loose, and colors clash,
My tapestry looks like a splash.
What once was grand, now looks bizarre,
Did I just weave a laughing star?

Every stitch a perfect jest,
Each knot reveals a funny quest.
I find a cat tangled in yarn,
Surprise! It's now a crafty barn!

Our lives, a fabric, tattered and torn,
Laughing at each frayed little scorn.
Unravel, unravel, let's see what's done,
Every twist brings giggles, oh so fun!

So let's embrace this funny shawl,
With pieces mixed, we'll stand tall.
In this absurd, chaotic dance,
We find delight in every chance!

Dreams on the Cutting Room Floor

Lights, camera, wait—who hit pause?
Scenes are missing, caused by flaws.
In the script, we had it right,
Now it's lost in the film's twilight.

Roll the tape, what's that bad take?
I mixed up dreams for pie and cake.
Chasing thoughts that flee with grace,
Laughing at this frantic race.

Who knew a sneeze could steal the show?
Or that a slip would steal the glow?
In the chaos of scenes we find,
The best of moments left behind.

So here's to dreams that went astray,
And to the fun in disarray.
For even in the crafty blurs,
We find the joy in all our purrs!

Paths Yet to be Trodden

In shoes too big, I take a stride,
My left foot's lost, I'm along for the ride.
With maps all scribbled and plans all askew,
I wander the road, just following you.

A squirrel drops nuts, as I trip on a stone,
I laugh at the chaos, I'm not quite alone.
With missing keys, I can't find the door,
What's open inside? Just stories and more!

Through alleys of giggles and gardens of green,
I chase after thoughts that are rarely serene.
With butterflies swirling and pies in the sky,
I'm piecing life's oddities, oh my, oh my!

So let's ride this carnival, up and down,
With hats that are crooked and smiles that astound.
The fun's in the journey, that much I can tell,
We might miss a few pieces, but we fit in well!

The Art of Missing Pieces

I bought a jigsaw, a sight of delight,
Opened the box, it was quite the fright.
There's a corner piece gone, I look for a clue,
Should I use some gum? Or maybe some glue?

My cat steals a piece and bats it away,
I'd chase him around, but I'm not here to play.
With puzzle in hand and a grin on my face,
I'll scribble some colors, like wild in a race!

The sky's now a purple, the grass glows in pink,
I venture to ponder, should I even think?
With laughter erupting, alongside all gaps,
The picture's a riot; my brain has mishaps!

So toast to the gaps and the quirks we embrace,
In a world that feels silly, I find my own space.
With colors unbound and laughter to share,
I might not have all, but I've got flair!

Whispered Longings

In a sock drawer, my missing mate,
Underneath a pile, it hides, it waits.
I often ponder where it went,
Did a hamster take it for a rent?

In the fridge, there sits a spare,
Could be a lid or a cat's lost hair.
The dog looks guilty, and I suspect,
He's the reason for all this neglect.

Mismatched pairs, a comic show,
Each new combo, a laugh to throw.
A shirt and a sock, in wild display,
Dancing together in bright array.

So I raise a toast to scattered bits,
And all the jumbles that life permits.
For in the chaos, joy ignites,
Like missing socks on lazy nights.

Jigsaw Pieces of Memory

A thousand pieces on the floor,
But which one goes where? I'm not sure.
Some fit together like old friends,
Others smirk, their fitting ends.

I twist and turn with furrowed brow,
As if the cat could show me how.
With a pounce, she scatters them wide,
Now it's a puzzle with a surprise ride!

Each forgotten corner has a tale,
Of missing links that wail and flail.
I giggle at the ones that fool,
Mixed up pieces inside the pool.

Shake the box, let's give it a whirl,
Amid the chaos, laughter unfurl.
After all, it's not the fit I seek,
But joy in madness, the happy peak.

The Threads We Leave Behind

A loose thread tangled in my hair,
A sign of chaos just floating there.
Did the cat play a careless game,
Or has my brain gone truly lame?

In the attic, old hats look on,
Each is grinning, now they've won.
They sport the quirkiest of styles,
Reminding me of my younger miles.

I'm seeking treasure in the mess,
Some old gloves and a purple dress.
Even if they don't quite match,
This style slip-up brings a patch!

So let the threads unravel slow,
Each one tells tales that brightly glow.
A laugh recalls a joker's spree,
In the threads, I find much glee.

Echoes of What Remains

A spoon's gone AWOL, where could it be?
Cereal with chopsticks, oh woe is me!
The fork's on the lam with mashed potatoes,
While the spatula hides with new housemates.

Echoes of dinner where laughter rang,
Now it's just me, with the fridge's clang.
The dog's judging from the floor below,
While I wonder what's left to show.

As the clock ticks on, I make a plan,
To summon the missing in our multi-pan.
For though they scatter and take their flight,
In memories, they still ignite.

So here's to the whims and quirky bits,
To all the moments that life admits.
Let's raise a fork to the lost and found,
In empty spaces, joy is profound.

Navigating the Abyss of Absence

In the closet, shoes do wander,
They pair up, but who knows the blunder?
Socks go missing, it's quite the scene,
With one of each, my foot's a machine!

I search for keys in the strangest places,
Under the couch, in pet's warm embraces.
They hide and seek, like a game for fools,
My car won't start; guess I'm skipping schools!

Old maps rolled up, with missing spots,
Directions they give, but they're all just dots.
I'm lost in thought, on this wacky quest,
For treasures unseen; oh, isn't it the best?

With a wink at the sun and a laugh with the breeze,
I dance on this path, catching moments with ease.
Embracing the strange and the things that abound,
In absence, there's humor, when silliness is found!

Threads of Hope in a Fraying Fabric

My sweater's lost buttons, oh what a sight,
A patchwork of colors, it's quite the delight.
Each thread tells a tale of misfits and blends,
I wear my mistakes; they're my cherished friends!

The quilt on my bed, with bits stitched in haste,
A jumble of memories, none going to waste.
With laughter it whispers, as blankets embrace,
In frayed edges, stories of warmth find their place.

A hat from last summer, oh what a goodbye,
Adventurous pigeons decided to fly.
With plucky resolve, I wear what I've lost,
For style's just a game; it's worth any cost!

In each thread a giggle, in patterns a cheer,
With every odd piece that hangs ever near.
In the fabric of life, let me drape my odd ways,
For hope finds its thread in the weirdest displays!

Fragmented Whispers

Memories flicker, like fireflies at play,
Some drift into shadows, while others stay.
I gather the pieces, as winks from the past,
In fragments of laughter, my joy holds steadfast.

Conversations started, then lost in the air,
I nod to the silence; we've both been aware.
Incomplete stories may sound like a tease,
But hey, they ignite my imagination with ease!

Friends pinball around like a game that's gone wild,
The jokes they once told make me feel like a child.
Yet when they depart, oh where do they roam?
In whispers we share, together, we're home.

Each laugh is a puzzle; a glorious mix,
From fragments of nonsense, it's all just a fix.
So let's dance in the chaos, with glee in our hearts,
For broken reflections are sometimes the arts!

The Sought-After Shades

Sunglasses lost, where could they have gone?
Under the sofa, or in the lawn?
A quest for style on a bright sunny day,
But I'm wearing last week's shades—hey, that's okay!

Tell me why they wander and leave me alone,
Dear shades, have you found a new place to roam?
In pockets, they're lost with an entire sock fleet,
The mystery thickens: is this life's little cheat?

I look in the fridge, might they be chilling there?
Or perhaps at the party, pretending to care?
But wherever they are, there's laughter to share,
For style's only missing when I'm unaware!

So I strut with my mismatched, half-hearted glare,
With a grin that says, "Hey, I don't have a care!"
In this silly fiasco, I find bright applause,
With every lost item, a pause and a cause!

Pieces in the Mist

In the morning, I search the floor,
For socks and more, there's never a bore.
My cat thinks it's fun to chase a sock,
While I trip on the crumbs near the clock.

The puzzle's half done, or so I think,
But where's that one piece? I'm on the brink!
Under the couch or lost in the chair,
Maybe it's hiding, just to be rare.

A drawer full of things, all mismatched and wild,
Like a toddler's art, it's chaotic and styled.
I laugh at the chaos, it brings me delight,
Perhaps the lost pieces are flying a kite.

So I grab a big bowl, and toss in what's due,
A game for the ages, or a riddle to chew.
With smiles and laughter, I gather my finds,
For missing a piece just sharpens the minds.

When Shadows Collide

In the kitchen, the shadows play,
Dancing around in a quirky way.
A fork with a spoon, they form a crew,
While a lonely knife feels left out too.

The sunlight beams in with a cheeky smirk,
As mismatched dishes begin to lurk.
Together they giggle, in perfect confusion,
Wishing for order in this grand illusion.

A cup on the shelf thinks it's quite slick,
But it falls right down with a terrible click.
A plate shatters dreams of a well-set table,
While cups form a band, oh so unstable.

But laughter's the glue that holds it all tight,
In this crazy kitchen, a silly delight.
When shadows collide, it's all just a show,
Embracing the chaos wherever we go.

Unsolved Wonders

The sock monster strikes when I least expect,
A twist in my tale, oh please, what the heck?
One foot in shoes, the other in air,
Who knew getting dressed could lead to despair?

The jigsaw sits quiet, pieces askew,
I can't find the edge; it's a real hullabaloo.
An elephant's trunk? No, that can't be right,
Or maybe it's something that's taken to flight.

A T-Rex with wheels? I can't even tell,
With one missing piece, it's a story to sell.
I laugh as I ponder this jumbled delight,
How fitting it is, everything feels light.

So here's to the wonders that baffle our days,
With missing links, we'll follow the maze.
In the chaos resides a curious zest,
For life's little puzzles, we all are a guest.

The Dance of the Lost

In a world where the missing pieces sway,
I follow their dance in a silly ballet.
A shoe on the left, a sandal on right,
They twirl in the twilight, quite a lovely sight.

The keys took a trip, left me in despair,
They're jiving with coins in the fluff of my chair.
A hat on the dog, oh what a surprise,
As they caper around with their whimsical ties.

The remote is a ninja, swift in its sneak,
Dodging my reaches, it's gone for a week.
Yet here I am laughing, with joy in my chest,
For missing a piece means there's more to ingest.

So let's toast to the lost, the odds, and the ends,
For they make the best stories, our quirky old friends.
In the dance of the lost, we find, oh what fun,
As we celebrate chaos, for all has begun.

The Places We Overlook

I searched for my keys in the fridge, oh dear,
A mystery that I hold so near.
The couch might just hide a lost sock,
Or maybe it's taken a stroll 'round the block.

My phone's misplaced in the laundry's embrace,
Could it be hiding in my old lunch case?
Each missing item, a tale all its own,
In this game of hide and seek, I've overgrown.

Books stacked high, but the shelf's a mess,
A treasure hunt leads to my old pink dress.
In every corner, a surprise might appear,
A long-lost treasure, or just last week's beer.

Have you seen my marbles? They rolled away,
Probably planning a bright sunny day.
Next time you lose something, don't fret or pout,
Just know it's off on adventures, without a doubt.

Moments Adrift

I dropped my sandwich while dreaming of lunch,
It fell on the floor with a big smelly crunch.
Time flew by while I played with my spoon,
Now I've lost track; is it morning or noon?

A sock on my hand became a strange glove,
I waved at my cat, said, "I'm doing great, love!"
The clock's ticking loud, but I'm in a trance,
Is today Thursday? Or was it just a chance?

My thoughts drift away like boats on the sea,
What was I saying? Oh yes, happiness spree!
Coffee is fine, but the milk went astray,
Perfectly normal, in my own quirky way.

But when moments drift, they bring laughter that's sweet,
Who knew being lost could be such a treat?
Each little mishap a story to tell,
In the chaos of life, I'm doing quite well.

Beyond the Visible

I peeked behind the curtain; what did I find?
A sock puppet party, oh, how unrefined!
They danced to the music of my old hair dryer,
And sang in harmony, oh, those sock-squire!

The dust bunnies staged their own little act,
They even held signs for some missing snacks.
Beyond what I see, there's a world full of fun,
Where mismatched oddities have just begun.

A lonely lightbulb put on a show,
With flickers and flashes, oh, how they glow!
These bizarre things make me giggle and snort,
There's more to discover in this silly court.

So if you look closer, don't shy away,
You might find surprises in light of the day.
In the quirks of the mundane, hilarity reigns,
Each odd little moment, a treasure that gains.

The Quiet Abandon

A banana on the couch? Now that's quite odd,
Was it lost in a discussion? I give a nod.
Leftover pizza, a mystery slice,
Who took the last bite? Was it cat or mice?

The remote's gone missing, oh, what a shame,
Was it my fault? Am I part of the game?
In each quiet moment, chaos thrives bright,
While there's laughter and mayhem concealed by the night.

Old projects piled high like a mountain of cheer,
Remnants of hobbies I started last year.
Sometimes it feels like I've grown quite a knack,
For biting off more than I can ever track.

Yet amidst the abandon, I find pieces of joy,
Each misfit and mishap, a riddle, a ploy.
So here's to the chaos, the giggles and sighs,
In the quiet abandon, my treasure lies.

Corners Unexplored

In the attic, dust bunnies roam,
Where half-baked dreams call home.
Forgotten socks have a dance,
While the cat tries to take a chance.

Boxes filed with things called 'treasures',
In the hunt, I find odd pleasures.
A jigsaw piece in a cereal box,
And I wonder, am I the fox?

Post-it notes from ages past,
Whisper tales too loud to last.
With crumbs of snacks on a shelf,
I laugh, as I can't find myself.

After searching with no fate,
I give in - why contemplate?
I'll make a feast from leftover bits,
And name it "Wonderful Misfits."

Reflections Without a Mirror

In puddles, I see a jumbled mess,
A quirky face, I must confess.
No mirror shines to help me peek,
But hey, I fancy being unique!

With every frown, a giggle starts,
Shadows dance like playful arts.
Who needs clarity or a guide?
I'll wear my wittiness with pride!

The sun beams down like a jester,
I chase my thoughts that want to fester.
But in the chaos, I've learned to bend,
And make a show of the blend.

So here's to all the flawed designs,
Each twist and turn like tricky lines.
I'll grin at gaps and misshapen views,
After all, laughter sees me through!

Emptiness Among the Full

Bottles lined up, each one a tale,
Yet one is missing, frail and pale.
A hero lost in a sea of cheer,
I chuckle softly – it's quite unclear.

Fridge full of food, yet I crave,
A chocolate bar that went to the grave.
Spaghetti stretched, all tangled and long,
I mimic my dinner with a silly song!

Friends gather round, pots all a-clatter,
But who took the cookies? Oh dear, what's the matter?
In plenty, we joke about what's amiss,
For 'little things' hold a comical bliss.

So lift your cup, let's toast to the twist,
To the things that vanish – how can we resist?
In gaps and laughter, we find our way,
Making sense of chaos, day by day!

The Incomplete Verse

Words half-formed, ideas that stall,
Like a game where I drop the ball.
Every stanza feels just like a tease,
A poet's block, a sneeze, if you please!

Once I wrote with flair and grace,
Now I'm lost in lexical space.
But with a chuckle, I scribble on,
For it's in the flaws, the fun is drawn.

Rhymes that stumble, rhythms that flop,
I laugh at these moments, I won't stop.
With mismatched thoughts and coffee stains,
A masterpiece grows from mundane chains.

So raise a toast to the unfinished art,
To every odd line that plays a part.
In laughter and quirks, the magic flows,
In the incomplete, a humor grows!

Threads Unraveled

I once had a shirt, full of flair,
But the buttons were gone, stripped bare.
Each time I wore it, a breeze would sneak,
Leaving me laughing, feeling quite chic.

My sock drawer's a circus, colors collide,
Odd ones in pairs, but we still take pride.
Dancing around, with one on my foot,
Giggles erupt, who needs a good suit?

A puzzle I made, but piece number four,
Is missing, I scowl, then laugh at the floor.
I'll craft a new picture, with glue and some glee,
Good enough for the cat, or just for me!

So let's wear our quirks, with wit and with cheer,
Embrace all the gaps, let's raise a bright beer.
With every slip-up, let's humor ignite,
For life is a riddle, and we're doing it right!

Echoes of the Unfinished

I started a novel, oh what a great tale,
But the plot took a turn, and I lost the trail.
Characters wandered, confused and bemused,\nNow
they're all napping, a bit overused.

An omelette I cooked, with flair in the pan,
But forgot all the eggs, oh where is the plan?
Just veggies and spices, a colorful mess,
Dining my best, what a hilarious guess!

In the garden I planted, seeds all a-jumble,
Weeds grew in vigor, but flowers may fumble.
I smile at the chaos, it feels like a dream,
Nature's own joke, just a topsy-turvy theme.

So here's to the moments, that don't quite fit,
The art of the missing, a whacky little hit.
Laugh at the echoes, of things left undone,
For in those bright gaps, we create our own fun!

The Silent Gaps

In my fridge there's a space, for fresh veggie treats,
But all I found there were some old, dusty beats.
A cucumber's lonely, a sad little chap,
Pondering why it's alone in the lap.

The sentences pause, like a sneeze gone awry,
Missing the punchline, oh my oh my!
Jokes left unspoken, a chuckle askew,
Laughter just echoes, in a room full of two.

My recipes skip, on a page all askew,
Butter turned bitter, what else is new?
A dash of confusion, a sprinkle of whim,
Sometimes the best meals come from daring to brim.

So let's toast to the blanks and the things that we lack,
With humor we light up the colors we track.
The silent gaps hold the laughter we seek,
In jest we find treasures, absurd and unique!

Portraits Half-Finished

I drew a fine portrait, but forgot the mouth,
The eyes are now glaring, holding their drouth.
With chalk in my hand, I giggle and say,
A mute masterpiece, hip hooray!

A canvas with colors, so bold and so bright,
But the sky's an odd shade—something's not right.
I point to the clouds, in a swirl and a spin,
It's all part of art, let the laughter begin!

My jigsaw's a picture, but where is the cat?
I'm left with a puzzle, a quirky format.
Friends gather around, to help fill the space,
Laughing and teasing, creating a race.

So let's paint with humor, let colors collide,
In portraits half-finished, creativity thrives.
With each brush and chuckle, the stories unfold,
In gaps, we find laughter, worth more than gold!

Vignettes of the Unattainable

I misplaced my socks again,
One's in the fridge, not in the den.
Coffee cup's always half full,
But can't find the spoon for my rule.

Jigsaw pieces stashed away,
Under the couch they seem to play.
Trying to fix a phone with glue,
Oops! Now it won't call or text you.

Chasing dreams with a rubber band,
How do I end up in no man's land?
Counting hours like they're confetti,
Late for the party—oh, isn't that petty?

A puzzle piece stuck in my shoe,
Stumbling around, what else is new?
At times it feels like a circus show,
But I'll laugh as I trip, just go with the flow.

Remnants of a Whirlwind

My breakfast flew off with a breeze,
Eggs are a mystery among the trees.
Chasing toast as it takes its flight,
Why is my kitchen a comic sight?

The vacuum's a monster, it lurks and hides,
Sucking everything, yet none of my pride.
Mismatched furniture, here and there,
Like an abstract painting made without care.

I've lost my keys in a sock drawer,
Who knew such chaos could make me roar?
Mail piling high in a tower so grand,
"Important stuff," yet it slips from my hand.

Dancing with dust bunnies on my floor,
They roll their eyes; they could ask for more.
Yet here we are, in a whirlwind's embrace,
Missing a few, but we still know our place.

The Missing Horizon

Sunrise is here, but the coffee's not,
Waking dreams in a forgotten spot.
Last seen chasing after the sun,
Maybe it's hiding, just having fun.

Clouds playing tag in the morning light,
Where'd I put my umbrella? Not in sight!
The horizon winks, it's a playful tease,
Like my cat who scampers and makes me sneeze.

Trying to assemble my thoughts today,
Each one seems to run away and play.
Navigating filters of dreamy haze,
I'll find it all after a few more 'la-la' days.

Chasing sunsets with a runaway shoe,
Why do my plans never stick like glue?
I'll laugh and wave as I miss a beat,
Gravity's pulling, yet I stay upbeat.

Shadows of Incomplete Thought

Thoughts wander off like a wayward pet,
One minute I'm clear, the next I forget.
Searching for answers in my backyard,
Found a lost sock, it caught me off guard.

Conversations fizzle like soda pop,
Lost the punchline, oh wait, does it stop?
Puns are lurking just out of reach,
They're like good advice, hard to teach.

I scribbled a note to remind myself,
But it's hiding under a book on the shelf.
Plans laid out like a treasure hunt,
Yet find myself stuck in a slippery front.

The fridge hums a tune, oh what's that sound?
It seems to giggle as I look around.
I guess we all dance in this quirky way,
Missing some pieces yet learning to sway.

The Grounds of Imperfection

In a garden that never quite grows,
Plants gossip about their absent toes.
The daisies chuckle, the roses sigh,
'Who needs a full bloom? Let's just try!'

Butterflies flit with a missing wing,
They dance around, pretending to sing.
With a flutter and flap, they turn to the crowd,
'Who needs perfect? We're still quite proud!'

The sun sometimes forgets to shine,
Casting shadows on a wobbly vine.
A squirrel pauses, eyeing a half-eaten nut,
'It's gourmet, I swear! Just a bit in a rut!'

Laughter echoes through this odd space,
In every crack lies a hint of grace.
For when pieces are lost, we find what's true,
Imperfection's charm is a splendid view!

Broken Reflections

I looked in the mirror, a funny sight,
With half my hair sticking up just right.
The other half, well, it chose to lay,
'Good morning, world! Let's seize the day!'

My shirt's buttoned up, but one is missing,
The other's through a hole, quite dismissing!
I grin at the chaos, let out a cheer,
'Fashion's a myth when you laugh in the mirror!'

My reflection winks, a jester in glass,
Says, 'You've got style, just let it pass!'
So I strut with flair, with bubbles and twirls,
Who knew being odd could get all the girls?

Every crack tells stories, sparkling bright,
A patchwork of joy, what a silly sight.
With mismatched socks and a crooked tie,
Who needs perfection? Just let it fly!

Unfinished Stories

There once was a tale, but oh dear me,
The pages are missing, where could they be?
A plot twist here and a hiccup there,
I guess we'll all just stop and stare!

Characters linger with nothing to say,
They chat about lunch, but what's the play?
The dragon forgot where it stashed its gold,
And the princess? She's just a bit too bold!

Once upon a time, adventures were grand,
Now they wander aimlessly, hand in hand.
When life scribbles notes instead of a script,
We turn coffee breaks into jokes well equipped!

Yet in this scribble, a beauty unfolds,
With laughter and whimsy, its warmth it holds.
So we pen our own tales, let wild thoughts burst,
Who needs the ending? The journey is first!

The Gaps We Bear

In a jigsaw with corners we can't quite find,
Those missing pieces, oh, what a bind!
We fumble and search, our patience wears thin,
But hey, let's just laugh; where to begin?

The cat sat on one, the dog chewed a side,
Still, we create magic, and let joy abide.
With colors and shapes that don't seem to fit,
We'll make our own fun in this quirky bit!

Sometimes it's chaos, a colorful mess,
We wiggle and giggle, who needs to impress?
With gaps in our stories, it's fully apparent,
That fun is contagious, and oh, so transparent!

So here's to our puzzles, the ones that we share,
With laughter and love, we lighten the air.
For every gap is a story to weave,
In this whimsical world, let's believe!

Searching for Lost Connections

I misplaced my phone again, oh dear,
It's like a magic trick, it disappears!
The clues are scattered, like crumbs in the air,
And here I am, searching everywhere.

My socks go one way, my keys take a flight,
Even my coffee has gone rogue tonight.
I call out their names, a comical sight,
Witty in my search, but feeling contrite.

Thought I'd found gold, a glittering thing,
But it's just an old penny, not much to bring.
With laughter, I sift through the whirlwind mess,
Life's little missing bits, I must confess.

Yet amidst all this chaos, I find some fun,
In searching for pieces, my race has begun!
So here's to the stuff that goes astray,
In the hunt for connections, I'll play all day!

The Space Where Joy Fades

There's a sock on the roof, is it trying to fly?
A lone little shoe says, 'Oh, give it a try!'
The sunlight's so bright, yet my humor's a bit hazy,
In the shadows of missing bits, I feel kinda crazy.

My cake has a layer that's sadly just air,
The balloons are deflated, they once danced with flair.
I'm chasing the laughter, but it runs from my grasp,
In this whimsical world, I wear a big gasp.

Cards on the table, only half of a deck,
Amused at the game, though it's all just a wreck.
With each missing piece, there's a giggle or two,
In the blank spaces, there's room to break through.

Hold on to the humor, let it help you mend,
What's lost isn't gone; it's a chance to extend.
We dance through the gaps, where joy tends to fade,
Finding laughter in puzzles, we joyfully wade!

Scraps of Time Left Behind

I found an old sandwich, ten days away,
Graced by the fridge, it's a true disarray.
Time slips through fingers like grains on the shore,
Each tick of the clock leaves me wanting for more.

A calendar's waiting, just teasing my mind,
With sticky notes placed, to help me unwind.
But where's all the time? Who'd loan me a bit?
These scraps I collect feel like dribs from a split.

To-do lists float like flimsy balloons,
Reminding me awkwardly, I'm juggling moons.
The deadline's approaching, what's left to define?
Just pick up the pieces and hope they align.

Through jumbled reflections, I chuckle and sigh,
Patchwork of moments that dance in the sky.
As I peer at the fragments, a smile does bloom,
In the hullabaloo, I'll find my own room!

A Symphony of Missing Keys

Oh, where did I leave my beloved set?
They're hiding like secrets, a little upset.
Piano's out of tune, can't find a sharp note,
A symphony's sound is afloat on a boat.

Crayons have skedaddled, they're painting the air,
A wild rendition of color and flair.
With laughter erupting as I take a look,
At the concert of clutter, life's own storybook.

I play with the whisk, pretending it's brass,
My cat's in the chorus, a comical pass.
The mobile of chaos is twirling just fine,
As I sway with the rhythm of my mismatched design.

So here's to the keys that wander away,
To the tunes that we chase in a fanciful way.
In the laughter that flows from this orchestral spree,
We dance through the gaps in our joyful decree!

The Puzzle of Silence

In the quiet, pieces roam,
A sock here, a shoe at home.
With every giggle, gaps appear,
Where did I put my missing beer?

I search the fridge and find a cat,
Why must it hide? Imagine that!
The remote's lost, the show's now begun,
Who needs control? Let's have some fun!

A half-eaten cake on the counter waits,
I count the candles, but not the plates.
Laughter echoes through the hall,
Where are the guests? They're lost in the thrall!

If pieces vanish, do we still play?
I'll grab a board game; let's stall the day.
The joy of finding is so divine,
Except when food is mysteriously mine!

Interludes of Absence

I look for joy in every crack,
Missed pieces bring me laughter back.
An errant shoe, a hidden hat,
Oh, the sights, just look at that!

The sun's in hiding, clouds above,
Yet under them, I find my love.
The dance of socks, a twirl of glee,
In every gap, there's room for me!

A sandwich made with mystery bread,
With every bite, a smile instead.
What's inside? A pickle surprise,
I never question; I just rise!

When guests arrive, they find my mess,
Where's the laughter? I must confess:
Without a clue, we spark delight,
In missing things, we thrive outright!

Finding Clarity in Chaos

In the whirlwind of my cluttered space,
The missing spoon starts a funny chase.
It hid behind a mountain of socks,
Who knew they'd be this sly as fox?

The laundry spins, it's quite a feat,
I'm losing track of all my heat.
Whose shirt is whose? Just take your guess,
The chaos brings its own success!

An empty box and tape galore,
'What was I wrapping?' I ask once more.
In the mayhem, a project waits,
Oh, how mischief often creates!

The joy is found in a careful glance,
Where things are lost, we twist and dance.
With laughter loud, confusion spins,
In each small gap, that's where it begins!

The Haze of What's Missing

I've lost my mind—not that it's rare,
Among my treasures, it's thin air.
What's behind that lurking chair?
Ah yes, my sanity's on a dare!

With every missing piece, I grin,
The hunt begins—let's take a spin!
Where did I leave my bright blue mug?
In all this haze, it's quite a shrug!

An unmade bed beneath the light,
Could it hold a secret? What a sight!
When cushions fly and laughs escape,
What's lost becomes a brand new shape!

A jumble here, a jumble there,
But missing things? I just don't care.
Let's crack a joke, raise up a cheer,
In every gap, adventure's near!

Missing Colors in the Picture

My canvas is all gray, no hue,
The sky is purple, it's true!
Where's the blue? Come on, paint!
I'll take a clown, or even a saint.

A splash of red, a hint of green,
This art's a mess, if you know what I mean.
The rainbow ran out, went for a snack,
Now I'm stuck with a monochrome track.

Can't find the yellow, it's gone astray,
Maybe it's hiding, just wanting to play.
Each stroke is a search, a colorful plight,
Let's paint with laughter, the canvas is bright!

With missing pieces, I laugh and grin,
A masterpiece, though, I'm in for a win.
Where's the missing colors, the vibrant cheer?
Hey little paint pot, come join the sphere!

Uncharted Paths of the Heart

Maps are amusing, with lots of lines,
But my heart's GPS can't find the signs.
It says turn left, I end up in town,
With ice cream shops, and clowns upside down.

Should I follow the river, or climb the hill?
Oh look, a signpost! (But it's just a grill.)
Roaming these streets with no plan in place,
I trip over shoes, can't find my grace.

Tinder's a map that leads me astray,
Swipe left, swipe right, oh what a fray!
Each heart a puzzle, with pieces so few,
Maybe I'll settle for pizza, that'll do.

Riding the waves of the sidetracked soul,
Finding direction, not searching for goal.
With laughter and fun, I'll steer the ship,
Charting the course with a chocolate chip!

Fragments of Yesterday

A missed birthday cake with candles all blown,
Forgotten my age, now feeling alone.
Snapshots of giggles, where did they go?
I can't find the pieces, but let's put on a show!

Woke up to find my socks don't match,
Searching for memories—what a strange batch.
Each fragment a puzzle, a whimsical spree,
I'll wear this weird mix, just let me be me!

Last week's dinner? I planned it with flair,
But ended with cereal, without any care.
Oh, the spaghetti that called for my name,
Now I'm left laughing at my culinary shame.

Dust off the past and let's make it bright,
These fragments of laughter, they'll feel just right.
We'll dance in the kitchen, while burning the toast,
Cherishing fragments, that's what matters most!

The Quest for Wholeness

Searching for socks, I find just one,
Not a complete pair, oh what fun!
Throw on some sandals, who needs a shoe?
I'll rock it with style, just watch how I do!

I'm on a quest for the missing piece,
Maybe it's hiding, won't you please lease?
A puzzle half-done, it's quite the delight,
I'll just add some glitter and call it a night.

Chasing my dreams, but I lost my way,
Rode a roller coaster, and now I'm in sway.
The goal is elusive, a runny old cheese,
With laughter and puns, I'll manage my ease!

Oh, wholeness is great, but I'll take the ride,
It's better with friends, let's enjoy this glide.
With jigsaw heartbeats, I'll find my way home,
In this wild, funny life, there's so much to roam!

Fractured Memories

When the cat wore my favorite hat,
I laughed so hard I almost sat.
Old photos, a strange game of charades,
Who's that guy in the sunglasses shades?

I trip on socks—some lost, some found,
The vacuum ate them, I'm pretty sure, drowned.
Baking fails that taste like a shoe,
Remembering a cake that once made me blue.

My youth in the attic, dusty and dim,
I swear that was a dress and not my gym.
Faded laughter echoes like a ghost,
Of all the mishaps, I cherish the most.

Fragments of tales once spun with delight,
Like a skit gone wrong on a mid-week night.
Silly memories, let's bring them alive,
Mismatched socks, the way to survive!

The Silence Within

In a room so quiet, you'd think it's a trap,
The silence whispers, 'Take a nap!'
I tried to count sheep but forgot the math,
A fuzzy llama joined my path.

The fridge hums a tune I can't quite catch,
Is that ice cream knocking? Oh, what a match!
The doorbell rings, but it's just a breeze,
Invisible friends, oh, how they tease.

Conversations with plants, they give me tips,
Telling me secrets with all their drips.
A cactus once bragged of its prickly stance,
"Come closer," it beckoned, "let's dance!"

These quiet moments, they tickle the bone,
Filled with laughter, I'm never alone.
With every silent giggle, I feel alive,
In this crazy hush, I brightly thrive!

Pieces Yet to Find

Searching for socks, oh, where do they hide?
A mystery buffet—come, take a ride!
Lego pieces lost under the chair,
An Indiana Jones with a plastic flair.

Dinner's a puzzle, which spice do I need?
"Just a pinch," they say, but I might exceed!
Sprinkle a dash, or was it a whole?
My kitchen's a chaos, like a rock 'n' roll role.

Puzzles on tables, they gather some dust,
Each piece whispers, "You've lost your trust."
That corner was easy, but this one has fled,
No one explained how to use my head.

Collecting oddities, things that don't match,
A slice of banana, and a salsa batch.
Living each moment feels just like a game,
And I need more pieces, but who's really to blame?

Glimpses of Life's Missing Scenes

In the backyard, the grass holds confetti,
A birthday long past, but the cake's still ready!
Whispers of laughter drift through the air,
Grandpa retells tales that were never quite there.

Zoom calls with filters, I'm a cat with a hat,
I'm trying to be serious, but I'm chasing a rat.
Oh, what a circus with faces so funny,
Are we all here, or is it just sunny?

Tea spills on napkins saved from the past,
Remember the time we thought it would last?
Photoshopped hugs are just pixels in space,
Wishing for moments—oh, what a race!

Glimpses of fun where whimsy grows wild,
Every blurred memory is like a lost child.
So let's dance in the rain, ignore the means,
With laughter and joy in these missing scenes!

Fragments Like Raindrops

A sock is lost, where could it roam?
The cat's got it, calls it home.
My keys are playing hide-and-seek,
While I'm just here, feeling meek.

The puzzle's bent, missing a smile,
A piece from last year's great big pile.
The fridge just laughed, it knows too well,
I'll scramble eggs instead, oh shell!

A shirt turned pink, the colors clash,
Washed with red—what a fashion smash!
My breakfast burned, the smoke alarm,
But hey, there's always room for charm!

In bits and bobs, humor's found,
With laughter's tune, the heart's unbound.
Embrace the quirky, the offbeat way,
Each forgotten piece, a brand new play.

Ghosts of the Unfathomable

I swear I put my phone right here,
It giggles back, just like a peer.
A ghostly wink from the missing toast,
Do I dare to search? I'm not that close.

My thoughts escape like butterflies,
They dance away, oh how they fly!
The cereal's a jigsaw—shapes and flakes,
A breakfast riddle, give me some brakes!

The cat's on the table, a curious thief,
Knocking my dreams—beyond belief!
My socks conspire, in pairs they cling,
A mischievous plot, what will it bring?

The ghosts of things, they haunt us still,
Whispering jokes, they tease and thrill.
So let's toast to the ghosts of the day,
Missing pieces can still join the play!

Whispers in the Void

I lost my pen in the coffee swirl,
It's drifting on dreams, in a cosmic whirl.
The left shoe's lonely, the right's gone spree,
An adventure waits, just not for me.

The fridge hums soft, dreams lost in chill,
Milk has left, what a sneaky thrill!
My to-do list sings a funny song,
It seems to know just where I belong.

The clock ticks loudly, won't let me snooze,
Reminding me of all I might choose.
Two left feet, I dance like a clod,
But what's this wiggle? A joyful façade!

Whispers from nowhere, they giggle and tease,
Maybe tomorrow, I'll find some ease.
With missing parts, I'll juggle and play,
Life's odd little quirks lead me astray!

The Unseen Connection

A sandwich made of air and dreams,
No pickles here, just silly schemes.
The chairs are deeply lost in thought,
Who said they'd join me? Turns out they ought!

Pots and pans like ducks in a row,
Stirring up trouble when I say hello.
The missing bits, the gaps in chat,
Have given way to a chubby cat!

The playlist skipped, oh what a treat,
It danced around on its little feet.
The bookshelf giggles, stories collide,
In the land of "Huh?", I take great pride.

Connections unseen, they weave and play,
Finding joy in a silly way.
With laughter loud, I'll piece this tale,
For every void has its own detail.

Unsung Notes in a Silent Symphony

In a concert hall where silence reigned,
A violinist played and the crowd was pained.
Without a bow, he strummed air with glee,
And claimed he was jamming with a ghost, you see.

The trumpets blared but forgot their tune,
A snare drum rolled, but napping by noon.
The conductor waved hands like a crazy bird,
While the audience laughed, not a note was heard.

A cello joined in, it was making a fuss,
But all it could touch was a nearby bus.
With each silent note, the laughter just grew,
In this symphony of giggles, what else could you do?

Finally, a sneeze like an oboe's high note,
Turned the whole crowd into a laughing boat.
In a world without sound, hilarity sings,
Who knew silent concerts could bring such bling!

Hues of an Uncolored Canvas

A canvas sat bare, waiting for art,
With brushes like ninjas and colors to start.
Except all the paints were missing their shades,
So the artist sketched cats in her playful parades.

With crayons of purple and a splash of bright green,
She made a blue elephant, quite unseen.
Stickers of stars danced alongside the lines,
While her masterpiece thrived on silly designs.

Across the blank page, the sketches took flight,
A squid wearing glasses, oh what a sight!
With smiles and laughter, the colors soon came,
From a feline ballet to a swirling cat game.

The hues may be missing, but who really cares?
Art is just laughter, with silly affairs.
A canvas uncolored is still full of cheer,
In the realm of imagination, there's nothing to fear!

Blurred Lines of Destiny

A road map was drawn with lines so hazy,
Destiny chuckled, thinking, 'That's crazy!'
GPS all tuned up but went on a spree,
Planned a trip to the moon, how far can it be?

Directions were mixed, it said, 'Turn left at the sun,'
Even a raccoon joined the fun, on the run.
With every wrong turn, the laughter would swell,
In a circus of chaos, they knew it too well.

They passed by a llama wearing a hat,
And a walrus that danced on a big ol' mat.
In the realm of detours, they laughed so hard,
Turns out the journey can be quite bizarre.

In this whimsical ride, knew they'd find fate,
Embracing each mishap, they just couldn't wait.
Blurred lines of life are a comical treat,
Here's to the laughter, now isn't that sweet?

Unraveling Forgotten Threads

A sweater once knitted with love and with care,
Was unraveling fast like it didn't quite care.
With each little tug, there came giggles galore,
As the knitter recalled how she made it, once more.

She found mismatched sleeves with colors that clash,
A pink one with polka dots, oh what a bash!
The yarn spun stories of laughter and cheer,
As the fibers of memories began to appear.

A cat chased a yarn ball, the traffic it caused,
With stitches a-flying, the threading paused.
But who needs a sweater when threads laugh and play?
In this wild little world, they refuse to decay.

So here's to the threads, they unravel with pride,
In the warmth of these moments, just take a ride.
For the mess is the magic that lights up the past,
And every loose end is a memory cast!

Emptiness Between the Stars

Stars twinkle, but one is shy,
Hiding behind clouds, oh why?
A cosmic game of peek-a-boo,
Just watch the sky for a silly view.

Galaxies filled with awkward gaps,
Some orbits wobble, others collapse,
Planets wander off the track,
Reaching for light but the humor's whack.

Contours of an Incomplete Picture

A canvas bright with random spots,
Brush strokes that dance but tie in knots,
Missing colors in a playful spree,
Artistry needs a proper decree.

Puzzles laid out with pieces stray,
Corners begging to find their way,
Shapes that giggle, refusing to fit,
The artist chuckles, 'Well, isn't this a hit?'

The Heart Against the Void

My heart beats loud in an empty room,
Echoes of love or perhaps just gloom,
Chasing shadows, but what a chase,
Falling in love, yet tripping in space.

Dancing alone with a comical twist,
Missing a partner, oh how I've missed,
But here I am, in rhythm and fun,
Even the void can't dampen this run!

Shadows Cast by Unfinished Dreams

Dreams loom large, yet some just float,
Like balloons that forgot to gloat,
They drift in a sky of whimsical blues,
Waiting for landings, they just refuse.

Chasing goals like a dog with a tail,
But some just wag and begin to fail,
Every attempt a twist of fate,
Who knew confusion could feel so great?

www.ingramcontent.com/pod-product-compliance
Lightning Source LLC
Chambersburg PA
CBHW070750220426
43209CB00083B/295